High-Stakes Careers

ER DOCTORS

Trudy Becker

Copyright © 2026 by Apex Editions, Mendota Heights, MN 55120. All rights reserved. No part of this book may be reproduced or utilized in any form or by any means without written permission from the publisher.

Apex is distributed by North Star Editions:
sales@northstareditions.com | 888-417-0195

Produced for Apex by Red Line Editorial.

Photographs ©: Shutterstock Images, cover, 1, 6–7, 8–9, 10–11, 14–15, 16–17, 19, 22–23, 26–27, 30–31, 32–33, 34–35, 36–37, 38–39, 44–45, 50–51, 52–53, 54–55, 56–57, 58; iStockphoto, 4–5, 20–21, 24–25, 40–41, 42–43, 46–47; Jose More/VWPics/AP Images, 12–13; Leonard Ortiz/Digital First Media/Orange County Register/MediaNews Group/Getty Images, 28–29; Ethan Miller/Getty Images News/Getty Images, 49

Library of Congress Control Number: 2025930329

ISBN
979-8-89250-668-7 (hardcover)
979-8-89250-702-8 (ebook pdf)
979-8-89250-686-1 (hosted ebook)

Printed in the United States of America
Mankato, MN
082025

NOTE TO PARENTS AND EDUCATORS

Apex books are designed to build literacy skills in striving readers. Exciting, high-interest content attracts and holds readers' attention. The text is carefully leveled to allow students to achieve success quickly.

TABLE OF CONTENTS

Chapter 1
SUDDEN SURGERY 4

Chapter 2
AT THE ER 8

Story Spotlight
PANDEMIC PROBLEMS 18

Chapter 3
ALL KINDS OF ISSUES 20

Chapter 4
UNCOVERING THE CAUSE 31

Chapter 5
CHALLENGES AND RISKS 40

Story Spotlight
READY FOR A SURGE 48

Chapter 6
BECOMING AN ER DOCTOR 50

SKILLS CHECKLIST • 59
COMPREHENSION QUESTIONS • 60
GLOSSARY • 62
TO LEARN MORE • 63
ABOUT THE AUTHOR • 63
INDEX • 64

Chapter 1

SUDDEN SURGERY

The doors of the emergency room (ER) burst open. Two EMTs push a stretcher inside. A boy lies on the stretcher. He is bleeding. A bone in his leg pokes through the skin.

EMTs use ambulances to rush people to hospitals for treatment.

ER doctors snap into action. The boy needs surgery right away. So, the doctors rush him to the operating room. There, they work to stop the bleeding. Nurses help. The team moves as fast as possible. The doctors put the bone back in place. Then they use stitches to close the wound and help it heal.

HEADS UP

While a patient is in an ambulance, EMTs call ahead. They let the hospital know that someone is coming. They give details about what is wrong. That gives ER doctors some time to get ready.

ER doctors may perform simple surgeries. For more complex operations, patients are sent to other parts of the hospital.

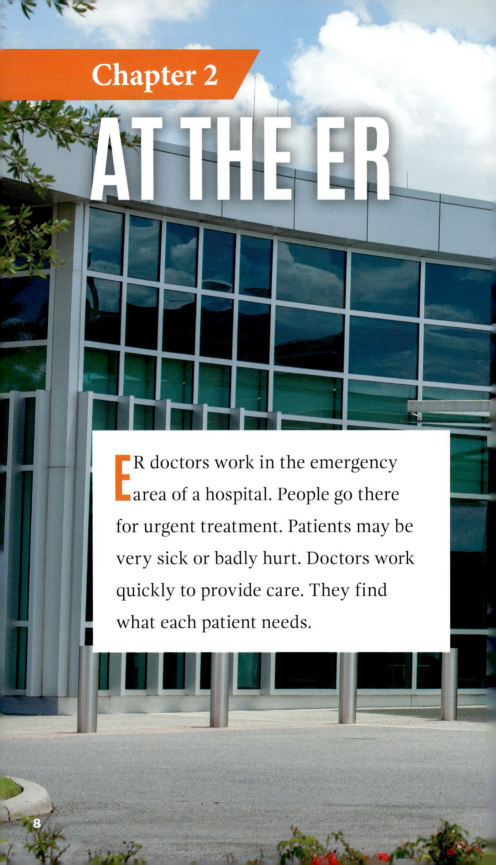

Chapter 2
AT THE ER

ER doctors work in the emergency area of a hospital. People go there for urgent treatment. Patients may be very sick or badly hurt. Doctors work quickly to provide care. They find what each patient needs.

Some hospitals use the term "emergency department" instead of "emergency room."

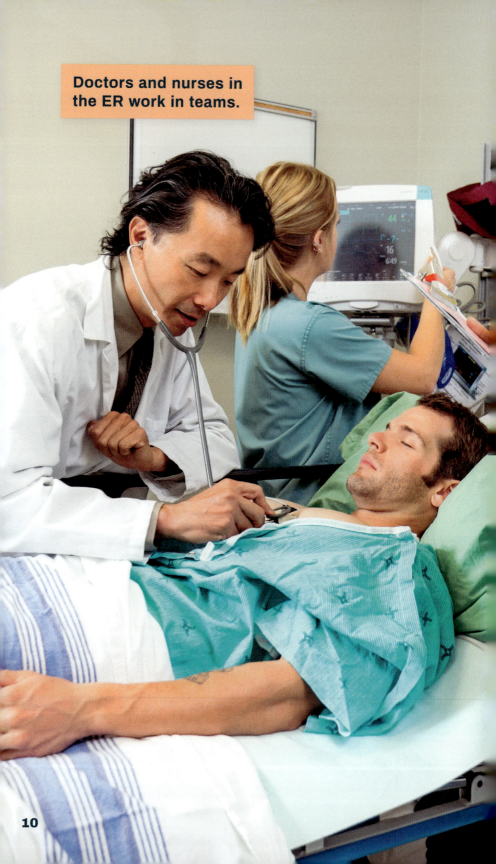

Doctors and nurses in the ER work in teams.

ERs stay open 24 hours a day. New patients can arrive at any time. So, ER doctors work in shifts. Some work during the day. Others take over at night. At each shift change, doctors have a quick meeting. The doctors who are leaving give notes about the current patients. They share what they have learned and what treatment people need.

TEAMWORK

Many health care workers help in ERs. EMTs bring new patients. And nurses provide many types of care. They treat wounds, give medicine, and check vital signs. They also get patients ready for doctors to see.

To treat patients, doctors often use a system called triage. Patients with the most-serious problems are usually seen first. Patients with problems that are not life-threatening may have to wait. This process helps doctors save the highest number of people.

After checking in, patients sit in a waiting room while doctors get ready to see them.

TRIAGE

Workers check each person who enters the ER. They see how much danger each person is in. They put patients in order for doctors to treat. Patients with serious problems often jump to the top of the list.

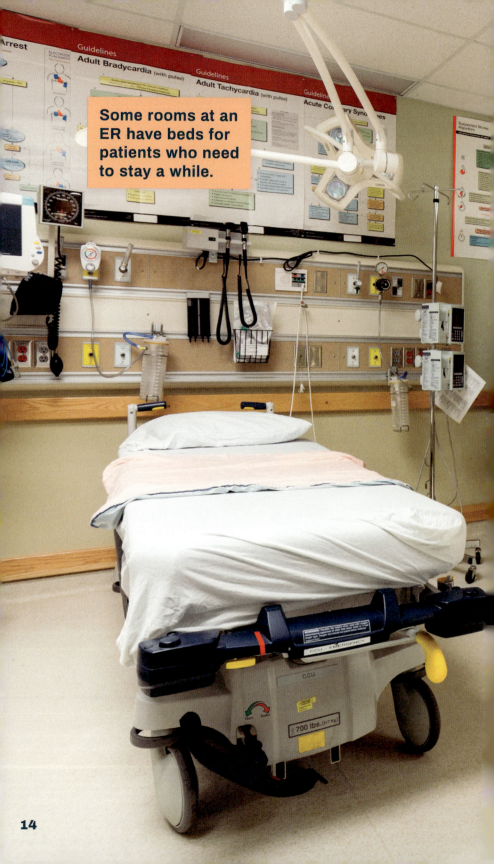
Some rooms at an ER have beds for patients who need to stay a while.

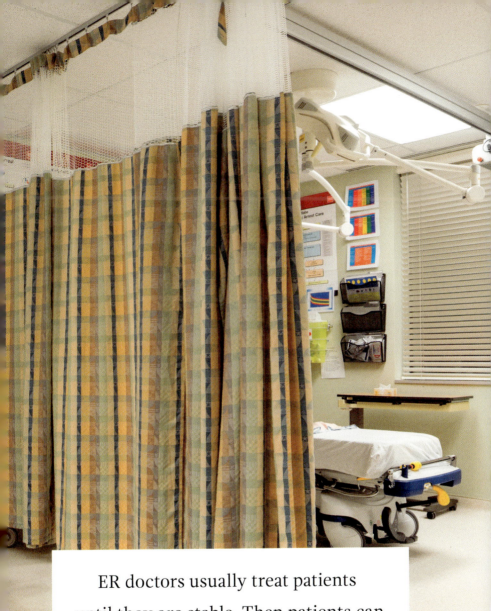

ER doctors usually treat patients until they are stable. Then patients can leave the ER. Some patients are ready to return home. Others still need help. They move to other parts of the hospital for more care.

On busy days, ER patients may end up waiting for hours to be seen.

Sometimes ERs get too full. That often happens during a surge. A surge is when many patients rush in within a short time. Doctors try to treat people quickly. But they may struggle to keep up. Wait times can grow long, even for more-serious problems. Doctors must think quickly to get people the help they need.

FAST PACE

The ER is often a very busy place. Doctors frequently have to multitask. They must be flexible, too. As things change and new patients arrive, doctors must adapt their plans. Staying calm under pressure is important. So is teamwork.

Story Spotlight

PANDEMIC PROBLEMS

In 2020, COVID-19 began spreading rapidly. Millions of people around the world caught the virus. Many became seriously sick. They rushed to ERs and hospitals. Doctors worked to care for them. But they faced many challenges. Some doctors got sick. And many hospitals ran out of beds for patients. Supplies were limited, too. For example, some patients needed ventilators. These machines help people breathe. But each hospital only had so many. Despite the challenges, doctors saved many lives during the pandemic.

During the pandemic, many people became too sick to breathe on their own.

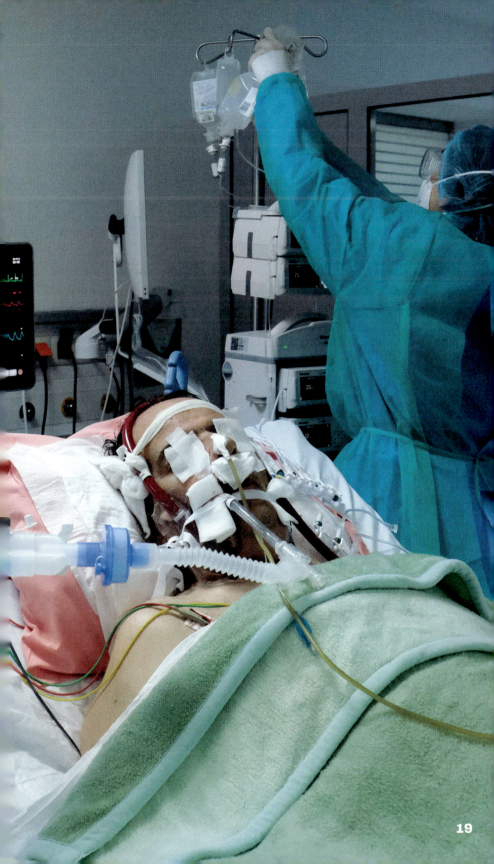

Chapter 3
ALL KINDS OF ISSUES

ER doctors see many different patients each day. Some patients' issues are obvious. Injuries are one example. Patients may have deep cuts. They may have bad burns. Bones may be broken, too.

In 2022, emergency departments in the United States had 155 million patient visits.

Doctors examine each injured area. They see whether wounds need stitches. They may also use X-rays to check for broken bones. If a bone is broken, doctors set it. They often add a cast to help it heal. Very bad breaks may require surgery.

BAD BURNS

ER doctors clean and bandage most burns. But some burns go very deep. For these burns, surgeons may need to do a graft. They cut away damaged skin. They replace it with skin from a different part of the body.

Slings, casts, and braces all help hold body parts still while breaks or sprains heal.

Other problems are harder to identify. Patients may feel sickness or pain. But they may not be sure why. Doctors try to figure out what is wrong. They ask patients to list their symptoms. Then they try to find the cause.

SEVERE SYMPTOMS

People often come to the ER with extreme symptoms. Some have terrible headaches or stomach pain. Patients may be throwing up. Or they may faint. Doctors and nurses work quickly. They try to help before symptoms get worse.

Stomach pain and nausea are some of the top reasons that people go to the ER.

Often, a symptom can have several possible causes. Shortness of breath is one example. It can be a sign of a heart attack. But pneumonia and asthma can also cause it. ER doctors rule out the most-serious problems first. They use tests and scans. They check for signs of big problems. If they don't find signs, they test for less-serious causes.

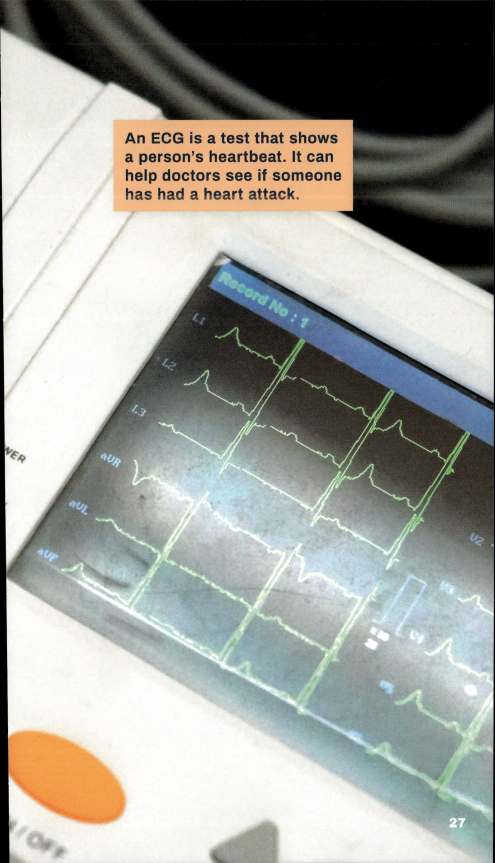

An ECG is a test that shows a person's heartbeat. It can help doctors see if someone has had a heart attack.

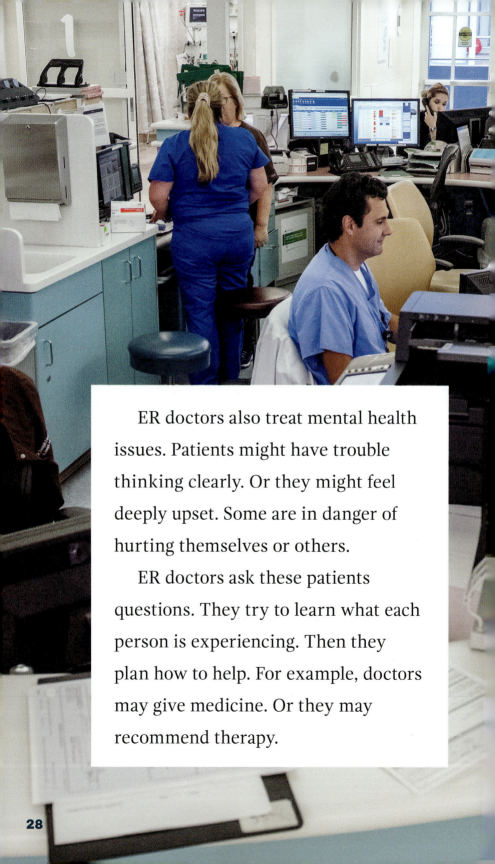

ER doctors also treat mental health issues. Patients might have trouble thinking clearly. Or they might feel deeply upset. Some are in danger of hurting themselves or others.

ER doctors ask these patients questions. They try to learn what each person is experiencing. Then they plan how to help. For example, doctors may give medicine. Or they may recommend therapy.

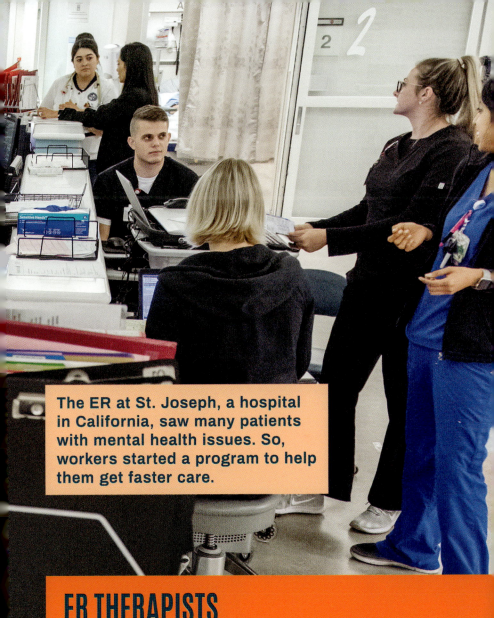

The ER at St. Joseph, a hospital in California, saw many patients with mental health issues. So, workers started a program to help them get faster care.

ER THERAPISTS

Many ERs have therapists. These experts specialize in mental health. They speak with patients in the ER. They help doctors learn what conditions a patient might have and what treatment could help.

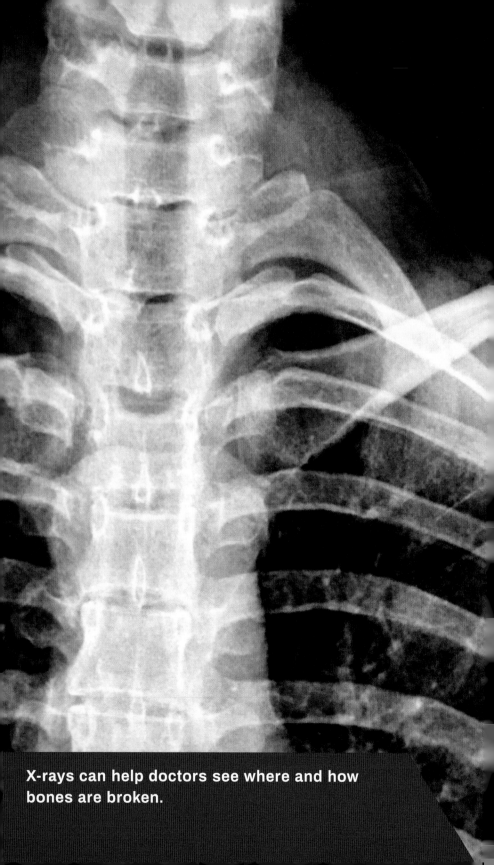
X-rays can help doctors see where and how bones are broken.

Chapter 4

UNCOVERING THE CAUSE

ER doctors must make fast decisions about what to do. Knowing an injury's cause helps doctors treat it.

For example, many people go to ERs because of falls. People who fall often hit their heads. They may have concussions. So, doctors check for this injury. They may use MRIs or other scans.

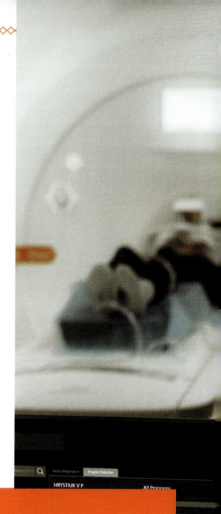

LONG FALL

In 2022, a Texas man was working on his house. His ladder slid. The man fell 30 feet (9 m) onto concrete. He broke many bones. He even went blind for a few days. But he lived. He stayed at a nearby hospital for more than a month.

An MRI scan can show damage to the brain or other tissues.

Some crashes involve dozens of vehicles. ERs may have to scramble to treat all the hurt people.

Car crashes also send many people to ERs each year. Crashes often cause deep wounds. Doctors rush to stop the bleeding. Crashes frequently hurt internal organs as well. So, doctors use scans to check for damage. They learn which parts of the body have been hurt.

ER doctors also care for people who have been shot or stabbed. These patients often bleed heavily. Doctors work fast so their patients don't lose too much blood.

Doctors also watch for warning signs of serious problems. For instance, heart attacks can be deadly. Doctors learn common symptoms of heart attacks. They also run tests to check people's hearts for damage.

Doctors start treatment for heart attacks as soon as possible. Medicine helps with pain and blood flow. Some patients also need surgery. Doctors cut into a person's chest. They open blocked areas in the heart.

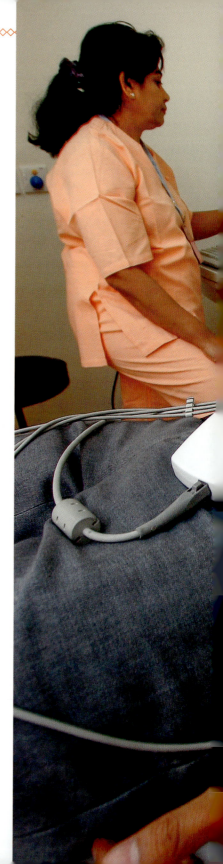

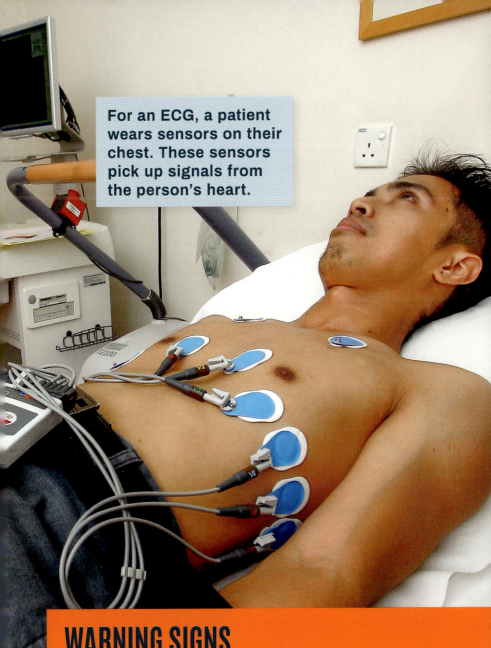

For an ECG, a patient wears sensors on their chest. These sensors pick up signals from the person's heart.

WARNING SIGNS

Many heart attacks cause chest pain. But there are other signs, too. People may feel dizzy or short of breath. Their stomachs may be upset. People may also feel pain along their arms, necks, or backs.

Early treatment is important for strokes as well. In a stroke, blood flow to the brain is limited or cut off. This kills brain tissue. Stroke patients may struggle to move, talk, or think. Some damage is permanent. But with quick treatment, patients may recover.

STUDYING STROKES

People can have several types of strokes. Each type needs different treatment. So, doctors do tests or scans to learn the type. Then, they can plan the best way to help.

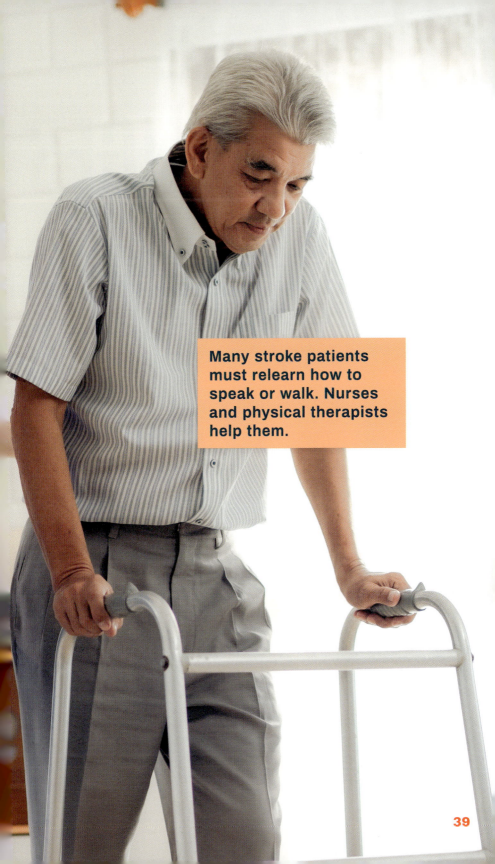

Many stroke patients must relearn how to speak or walk. Nurses and physical therapists help them.

Chapter 5

CHALLENGES AND RISKS

Being an ER doctor is very challenging. The number and type of patients is constantly changing. ER doctors must keep track of many details. They may work long shifts with few breaks.

On a busy day, an ER doctor may see more than 20 different patients.

Many patients are in serious condition. If doctors are too slow, a patient could die. However, going fast can be risky, too. Rushing makes mistakes more likely. And mistakes could harm patients.

To help, ER doctors use tests and scans. They check their ideas about what might be wrong. This helps make sure patients get the right diagnosis. Even so, doctors may miss problems. Or they may not be able to help in time.

Doctors may have to share bad news with patients' family members.

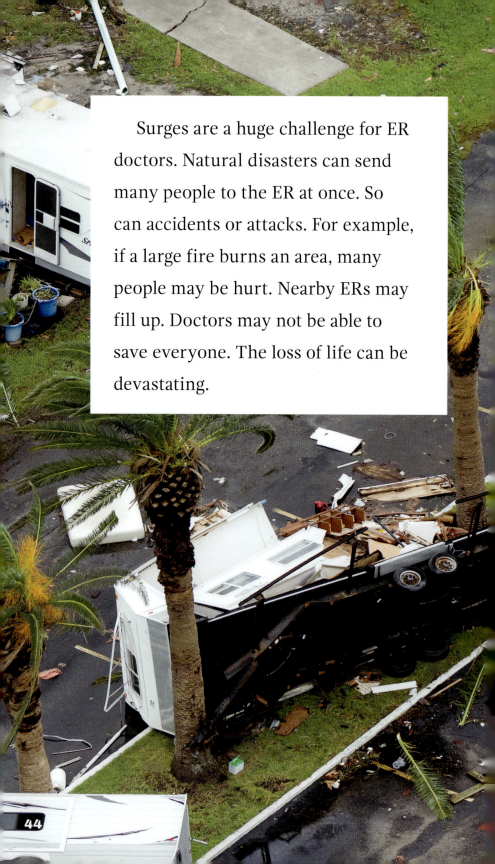

Surges are a huge challenge for ER doctors. Natural disasters can send many people to the ER at once. So can accidents or attacks. For example, if a large fire burns an area, many people may be hurt. Nearby ERs may fill up. Doctors may not be able to save everyone. The loss of life can be devastating.

MASSIVE CRASH

In 2005, thick fog drifted over a highway in Ingham County, Michigan. An SUV crashed. Other drivers couldn't see it. They crashed as well. About 200 cars piled up. More than 35 people got hurt. And two died.

Hurricane Harvey hit Texas and Louisiana in 2017. ERs saw a surge in patients after the storm.

ER doctors see lots of sick people each day. They can be exposed to many diseases. To stay safe, doctors wear protective gear. Gloves and masks are two examples. They help block germs. Even so, ER doctors sometimes catch illnesses from people they care for.

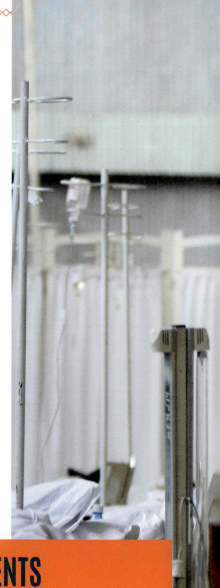

DANGEROUS PATIENTS

Patients in the ER are under a lot of stress. Many are very upset. Some may become violent. People may try to attack doctors or nurses. They may hit, kick, or punch.

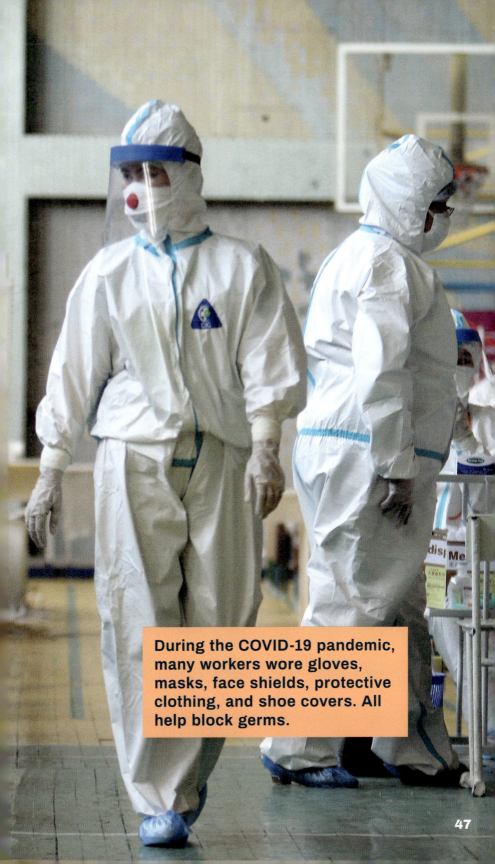

During the COVID-19 pandemic, many workers wore gloves, masks, face shields, protective clothing, and shoe covers. All help block germs.

Story Spotlight

READY FOR A SURGE

In 2017, a big country music concert took place in Las Vegas, Nevada. One man fired a gun into the crowd. He shot hundreds of people. Many were rushed to the ER at Sunrise Hospital.

When the first patient arrived, the ER's staff learned about the shooting. They got ready for a surge. They prepared operating rooms. And they called more than 300 doctors and nurses to come help. They planned ways to treat wounds and stop bleeding. Their actions saved many lives.

> The gunman at the Las Vegas concert killed 60 people and hurt more than 500 others.

Chapter 6
BECOMING AN ER DOCTOR

It takes years of training to become an ER doctor. First, people attend college. They often study biology or another type of science.

Next, people go to medical school. This usually takes about four years. Medical students take many classes. They learn about different diseases and injuries.

People who want to become doctors study anatomy. This type of science focuses on the parts of the body and how they work.

Medical students also practice taking care of patients. They do rotations. Students work shifts at hospitals or clinics. They practice diagnosing and treating real people. Teachers and experienced doctors help.

ROTATIONS

Most medical students complete several rotations. Each one lasts a few weeks or months. Some rotations take place in an ER. Others involve different types of care. For example, students may learn about radiology or caring for kids. This helps students build skills they may need in the ER.

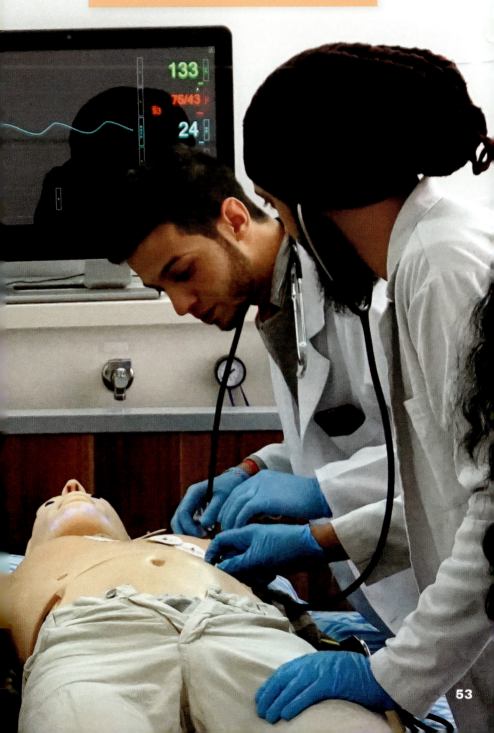

Medical students often practice on dummies before giving treatment to real people.

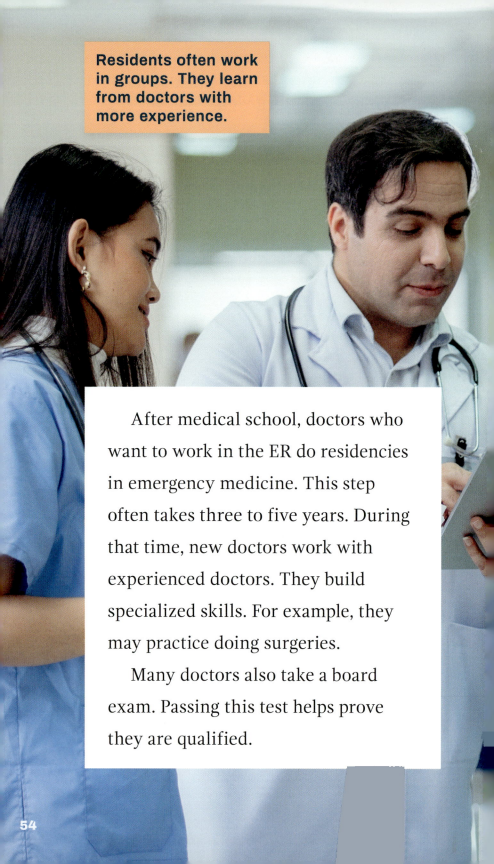

Residents often work in groups. They learn from doctors with more experience.

After medical school, doctors who want to work in the ER do residencies in emergency medicine. This step often takes three to five years. During that time, new doctors work with experienced doctors. They build specialized skills. For example, they may practice doing surgeries.

Many doctors also take a board exam. Passing this test helps prove they are qualified.

BROAD KNOWLEDGE

Many doctors are specialists. That means they work with one type of issue. For instance, some doctors treat eye problems. Others focus on bones. ER doctors often treat many types of problems. So, they need more general knowledge and skills.

After residency, people can work as ER doctors. But some choose to continue their training. They may do fellowships. These positions help them practice even more types of care. For example, some doctors train to use tools such as ultrasound. Others study trauma. They learn ways to treat serious injuries. This helps them prepare for the many needs that ER patients might have.

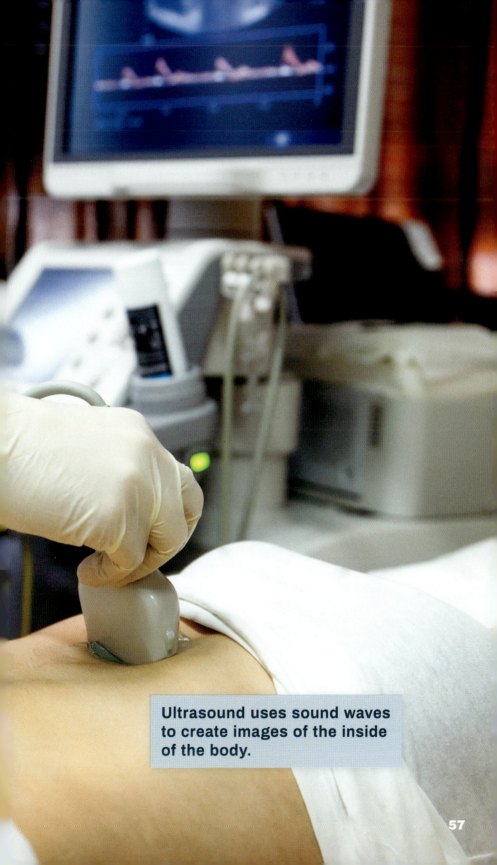

Ultrasound uses sound waves to create images of the inside of the body.

57

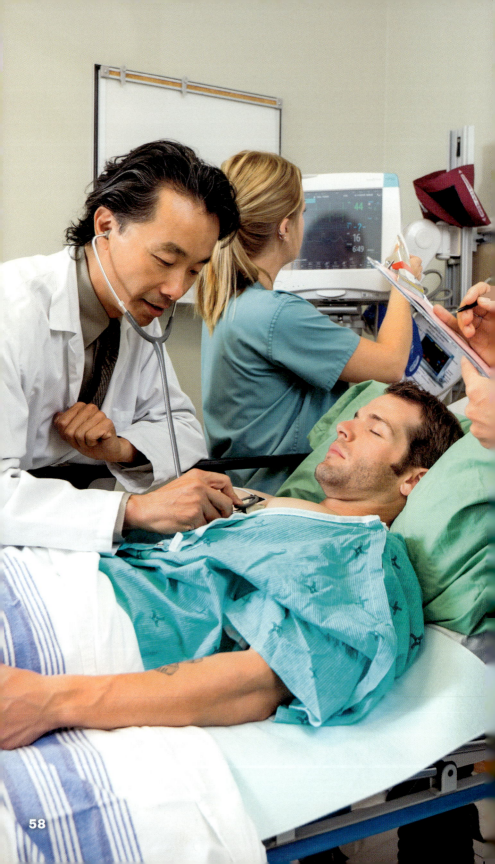

✓ SKILLS CHECKLIST

- Communicating well with others

- Diagnosing common diseases

- Reading X-rays and test results

- Setting broken bones

- Thinking quickly under pressure

- Treating deep cuts and burns

COMPREHENSION QUESTIONS

Write your answers on a separate piece of paper.

1. Write a few sentences explaining some of the challenges that ER doctors face.

2. Would you want to be an ER doctor? Why or why not?

3. What is one event that could cause a surge in an ER?

    A. a person falling off a ladder
    B. a large fire burning an area
    C. one car crashing

4. How could rushing lead to more mistakes in the ER?

    A. Doctors might gather too much information.
    B. Doctors might miss important information.
    C. Doctors might spend too long with each patient.

5. What does **urgent** mean in this book?

   *People go there for **urgent** treatment. Patients may be very sick or badly hurt. Doctors work quickly to provide care.*

   A. not very important
   B. needing help right away
   C. taking a long time to plan

6. What does **stress** mean in this book?

   *Patients in the ER are under a lot of **stress**. Many are very upset.*

   A. feelings of love
   B. feelings of worry
   C. peace and calm

Answer key on page 64.

GLOSSARY

concussions
Brain injuries that are usually caused by blows to the head.

conditions
Sicknesses or other problems that keep the body from working well.

diagnosis
The naming of a patient's health problem.

EMTs
People who are trained to give medical care during an emergency.

heart attack
A time when the flow of blood through the heart is blocked or stopped.

mental health
How well or unwell someone's mind is.

pandemic
A time when a disease spreads quickly around the world.

patient
A person who receives medical care.

radiology
Using and reading X-rays and other scans.

stable
No longer in an emergency.

vital signs
Measurements of the body's basic functions, such as breathing or heartbeat.

TO LEARN MORE

BOOKS

Kurtz, Kevin. *The Future of Medicine.* Lerner Publications, 2021.

Micklos, John, Jr. *Unusual Medicine.* Capstone Publishing, 2021.

Miller, Marie-Therese, PhD. *Jobs in Health Care.* Abdo Publishing, 2024.

ONLINE RESOURCES

Visit **www.apexeditions.com** to find links and resources related to this title.

ABOUT THE AUTHOR

Trudy Becker lives in Minneapolis, Minnesota. She went to the emergency room once for a scratched cornea.

INDEX

ambulance, 6

board exam, 54

COVID-19, 18

diagnosing, 42, 52

EMTs, 4, 6, 11

heart attacks, 26, 36–37
hospitals, 6, 8, 15, 18, 32, 48, 52

injuries, 20, 22, 31–32, 50, 56

medical school, 50, 52, 54
medicine, 11, 28, 36
MRIs, 32

operating rooms, 6, 48

pain, 24, 36–37
pandemic, 18
protective gear, 46

residencies, 54, 56
rotations, 52

sickness, 8, 18, 24, 46
strokes, 38
surgery, 6, 22, 36, 54
surges, 17, 44, 48
symptoms, 24, 26, 36

trauma, 56
treatment, 8, 11, 29, 36, 38
triage, 12–13

ventilators, 18

ANSWER KEY:
1. Answers will vary; 2. Answers will vary; 3. B; 4. B; 5. B; 6.